CONTENTS

The Opera House . 2

The Gardens 8

The Harbour . . . 14

Darling Harbour . 26

The City 32

The Beaches 40

The Bush 48

The Opera House

In the centre of Sydney, glistening in the sunshine, is a sculpture called Sydney Opera House. To visit one of the world's great buildings is more than just a visual fantasy, it's an experience to savour and enjoy. The sight of those soaring white sails is enough to make you want to sing with joy, to walk the ramparts of the podium is like strolling the deck of an ocean liner, and to enter the cavernous foyers beneath the shells you feel the same sense of awe as walking the aisle of a gothic cathedral.

Sydney Opera House is an extraordinary building and it has an extraordinary story. Danish architect Jorn Utzon won the design competition for the building in 1957. The cost was estimated at $7 million and it was expected to take three years to build. Fifteen tumultuous years later Sydney Opera House was completed at a cost of $102 million. Halfway through construction, Utzon resigned without leaving completed drawings of the theatres, so while the outside is Utzon's, the interiors were designed by an Australian architect, Peter Hall.

Guided tours of the Opera House theatres leave approximately every half an hour, seven days a week, from the lower concourse walkway on the southwest side of the Opera House. Backstage tours take place on Sundays.

Previous page: *Fireworks to celebrate the Centenary of Federation on New Year's Eve 2000.*

Above left: *A sculpture by the sea, the Opera Theatre shells of Sydney Opera House.*

Left: *The Opera House shells stand out like snow-capped mountains against black summer storm clouds.*

THE OPERA HOUSE

Left: Lighting creates a mood, in this case a warm yellow during the Festival of Sydney.

Below: Even with white floodlighting Sydney Opera House looks magnificent.

Below: Multicoloured lighting on the Bennelong Restaurant brings to mind the flower-power days of the sixties.

Above right: Red lighting and a full moon shining through clouds gives the Opera House a brooding, sinister feel.
Above: Cold blue lighting during the Sydney Olympics seems to capture the building's Scandinavian origins.

SYDNEY

Left: *Foyers with glass walls have sweeping harbour views.*

Left: *Flights of stairs lead from the northern foyers to the bar areas.*

Below: *The Concert Hall seating.* Above: *Passages beneath the shells.*

Previous pages: *An aerial view of the shells. The total order of tiles for the building including a margin for breakage was 1,044,250, every one 'marked with the signature and stamp of the architect'.*

THE OPERA HOUSE

Left: *The Opera House profile is a change from the ragged skyline of other city buildings.*

Below: *The harbourside broadwalk.*

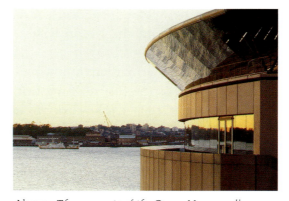

Above: *The ramparts of the Opera House podium.*

Right: Utzon used the broad stairs because 'When you see a hill before you, you want to climb up it, and so I put the wide steps in front of people leading into the foyer'.
Above: *Lights with spherical glass shades line the boardwalk.*

The Gardens

A minute's walk from the steps leading up to the Opera House is the entrance to Sydney Royal Botanic Gardens. The Gardens, one of the oldest Botanic Gardens in the world, was established in 1816 by a Scotsman, Governor Macquarie, when he appointed Charles Fraser, a soldier from his 46th Regiment of Highlanders, 'Superintendant of the Botanic Gardens'.

Fraser enthusiastically collected plants and seeds from Australia and the islands of the Pacific and exchanged plant specimens with overseas botanists to establish the Gardens. This work was carried on by succeeding Superintendants, one of whom, Richard Cunningham, had the misfortune to be speared to death by Aborigines while collecting plant specimens on the Bogan River during Thomas Mitchell's Australian expedition of 1835.

The Gardens were renamed the Royal Botanic Gardens following the visit of Queen Elizabeth in 1954. She was the first reigning British monarch to visit Australia. Near the point where she first stepped ashore, on the east side of Farm Cove, a wall is decorated with the royal crest to commemorate the event.

From the gate to the Gardens near the Opera House a little motorized train takes visitors on conducted tours of the Gardens. If going by foot it's a good idea to head for the centre of the Gardens where guide maps are available from the shop behind the kiosk. After wandering the Gardens, which are absolutely delightful, follow Farm Cove round to Mrs Macquarie's Point which has a view directly across to Sydney Opera House and the Harbour Bridge.

Above: *The Palm Grove, established in 1853, contains over 100 species of palms.*

Left: *The Palace Garden, near the Macquarie Street entry to the Gardens.*

Right page: *A view of the Gardens from Farm Cove with the Mitchell Library and Sydney City in the background.*

THE GARDENS

SYDNEY

Previous pages: *The Royal Botanic Gardens line the shore of Farm Cove.*

Below: *'The Hunter' in the Gardens.*

Above: *Hyde Park.*

Above left: *This sandstone folly is a replica of the Choragic Monument of Lysicrates in Athens.*
Above: *Venus de Milo in the Gardens.* Right: *One of a pair of bronze lions at the entry to the Azalea Garden.*

THE GARDENS

Left: *The sundial in the Herb Garden of the Royal Botanic Gardens. Taken just after midday in late winter according to the shadow.*

Right: *Paths meandering through the Gardens offer glimpses of Sydney Opera House and the harbour.*

Above left: *Elizabeth Bay House (1838) from McElhone Reserve. Designed by architect John Verge, the house was once considered the finest in the colony. Open daily to the public.* Above: *The Azalea Garden in the Royal Botanic Gardens.*

The Harbour

The word 'harbour' conjures up visions of ships unloading at docks and factories by the waterside surrounded by murky water with a colourful sheen of oil floating on the top. While Sydney Harbour certainly has docks and factories, much of the 160 kilometer shoreline is devoted to parks and reserves, and the water is *clean*. They even swam the Olympic Triathlon in it. I remember one morning I was photographing the Opera House from Dawes Point when I heard a splashing and was surprised to see a seal playing in the harbour.

There are many contrasts to be found around the harbour shore. Where the breezy towering cliffs of North Head guard the harbour entrance ocean swells send up a plume of spray as thay crash on the rocks. While at Bantry Bay and on the Lane Cove River the harbour waters lap gently at the roots of tidal mangroves. In one reach of the harbour you'll find quiet Store Beach and Collins Beach, accessible only by bush track or boat, which haven't changed in appearance since aborigines roamed the shore to prise oysters from the rocks. In other places the mood is more frantic, like at the harbour beaches of Manly Cove and Balmoral, where an ice-cream or a meal of fish and chips is only a walk across the street away.

For something quite different you can return to nature at the nudist beach of Lady Bay, or become a castaway for the day at the parks on Clarke, Shark or Rodd Island, where on a weekday you'll probably have the whole place to yourself.

The easiest way to get about the harbour is on one of the many ferries that ply the waters. Timetables are available at the ferry wharves at Circular Quay. The chances are your destination is only a short walk from the nearest wharf.

Above: *Part of the convoluted 160 kilometer shoreline of Sydney Harbour. This is Middle Harbour.*

Left: *February is the busiest season for visiting ocean liners. The 'Crystal Harmony' is moored on Sydney Cove as the 'Arcadia' passes the Opera House. From Quay West Suites.*

Right: *Mosman Ferry wrinkles the waters of Mosman Bay as she embarks for Sydney.*

THE HARBOUR

SYDNEY

Below: *The full-rigged Russian ship 'Palada'.*

Above: *The 'Bounty' of 'Mutiny on the Bounty' fame.*

Previous pages: *Stadium Australia from the observation deck of the Novotel, Homebush Bay.*
Centre: *Captain Cook's 'Endeavour' visits Sydney.* Above Left: *The 'Endeavour' on Sydney Harbour.*
Above: *The Mexican barque 'Cuauhtemoc' off Darling Harbour during a visit to Sydney.*

THE HARBOUR

Below: The small twin-hulled ferry 'Scarborough' dwarfed by the great span of Sydney Harbour Bridge.

Above: Manly ferries crossing on the eleven kilometer journey between Circular Quay and Manly Wharf.

Above right: The 'Scarborough' again, this time on the Lower North Shore run.

Above: All change at Circular Quay. In dock at the Overseas Passenger Terminal is the former P&O liner 'Canberra'.

19

SYDNEY

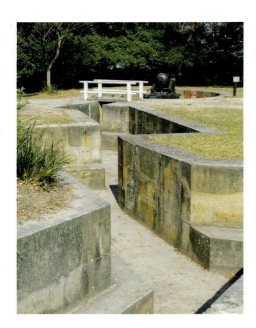

Far left: *Middle Head Fort.*
Below left: *Fort Denison.*

Left: *The elephant enclosure at Taronga Zoo.*

Above: *At least the giraffes seem to appreciate the view.*

Previous pages: *Fireworks for the Olympics Closing Ceremony.*
Above: *Lush vegetation surrounds homes on the harbour at Seaforth.*

THE HARBOUR

Following pages: The 'QE2' docking at Sydney Cove as the 'Russ' passes beneath Sydney Harbour Bridge.

Left: The liner 'Switzerland' is dwarfed by the great monolith of Sydney Opera House.

Right: This time it's the Opera House that's dwarfed by the giant liner 'Crystal Harmony'. From Quay West Suites.

Above left: The 'Club Med 2' at Circular Quay. Like some of the first powered ships to enter Sydney, the Club Med has sails as well as an engine.
Above right: The P&O sister ships 'Pacific Princess' and 'Island Princess' in company on the harbour.

Darling Harbour

Darling Harbour immediately west of the City *was* once an industrial site. Factories, docks and a power station lined the shore, a constant stream of traffic thundered over Pyrmont Bridge and at the head of Cockle Bay a network of railway tracks serviced woolstores, food markets and a meat cold-storage plant. By the early 1980s most transport had switched from the railways to the roads and the site was largely derelect.

Sydney Council had Darling Harbour earmarked for parks and housing when the State Premier suddenly announced it was to be a recreational 'people's place' of shopping centres, restaurants, museums and a casino connected to the city by a monorail. Special Legislation was enacted to steam roller the project through over the objections of Sydney Council so construction could be completed in time for the Bicentenary in 1988.

The result is a happy transformation of an urban space. The National Maritime Museum and Sydney Aquarium stand on either side of Cockle Bay, linked by Pyrmont Bridge which is now reserved for pedestrians. The city traffic is carried out of harm's way on the elevated Western Distributor running through the center of Darling Harbour which adds a kind of sculptural element to the scene. On Pyrmont Bay, just round from the National Maritime Museum stands the monolithic Star City Casino, looking a little like Pyrmont Power Station which it replaced. To keep Sydney Council on speaking terms, outside the Exhibition Centre a park and Chinese Gardens were included in the design.

Above right: *The Aviation and Space exhibit, one of the many displays in the Powerhouse Museum. The Museum occupies the former Ultimo Power Station, which generated electricity for Sydney's tram system.*

Right: *Yachts on Cockle Bay at Darling Harbour during the Sydney Boat Show.*

DARLING HARBOUR

Above: The National Maritime Museum focuses on the history of Australia's links with the sea.

Above: An avenue of palms flanks the path to Tumbalong Park.

Right: The biggest ship in the museum's collection is the former RAN destroyer 'Vampire'.

Above: Sydney's Panasonic Imax Theatre has the world's biggest movie screen.
Above right: Sydney Exhibition Centre has Australia's largest column free exhibition space.

SYDNEY

Previous pages: *An aerial view of Darling Harbour.*

Above: *Sydney monorail outside Harbourside shops.*

Left: *Crossing Pyrmont Bridge. The white Four Points Hotel and Sydney Aquarium are behind the train.*

Above: *Sydney Light Rail.* Above right: *The monorail at Convention Station.*

Darling Harbour

Left: *The fountain at Cockle Bay Wharf.*

Below: *Pyrmont ferry wharf.*

Above: *Star City Casino.*

Above: *The 'Garden of Friendship' is the largest Chinese Gardens outside China.*
Right: *Cockle Bay Wharf contains a variety of restaurants and bars.*

The City

If there was a movie title that sums up the City of Sydney it would surely be 'The madness of King George'. Sydney is a beautiful lady without mercy, capricious, eccentric, irreverent, even a little… mad. George III, a devoted father and husband, was conscientious in his regal duties, taking an active hand in government by appointing his own ministers. Following the loss of the American colonies in 1783, England was casting about for new territories so dispatched a small fleet of ships to populate an empty land on the other side of the globe with criminals. An act of madness if ever there was one. The First Fleet's destination, Botany Bay, was swampy and had no running water, so they upped anchor and settled instead at the next harbour to the north. There, on a little cove, the English flag was raised, and Governor Phillip christened his new camp 'Sydney', after George Rose (Lord Sydney), the Secretary for Home and Colonial affairs who was responsible for the foolhardy venture. The year was 1788, the same year that King George became mentally deranged. Perhaps the thought of colonizing a continent six months journey away by sailing ship had played on his mind.

The main road through the town was later named George Street after the good king. If you follow its erratic course to Hay Street and turn right to the Powerhouse Museum, inside you'll find an original Boulton & Watt steam engine. It was installed at Whitbread's Brewery in London, where in 1787 Samuel Whitbread proudly showed to King George 'this Engine which performs the work of 35 Horſes'. A tangible link with our past, it also ushered in the mad machine age we now live in.

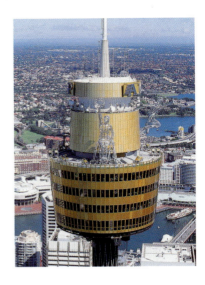

Above right: *Sculptures of athletes were mounted on AMP Tower for the Sydney Olympics. The tower, rising 1,000 feet (305 meters) above street level, has an observation deck and revolving restaurants at the top.*

Right: *An aerial view of Sydney Central Business District. Separating Hyde Park on the left and the Domain on the right are the twin spires of St Mary's Cathedral.*

Right pages: *The Rocks was the first area of European settlement in Sydney.*

THE CITY

Left: Houses on Argyle Green date from the 1840s to the late Victorian era.

Above: A hotel and shops on George Street face towards First Fleet Park.

Left: Lower Fort Street from Observatory Hill. A small fort called Dawes Point Battery was demolished when the Harbour Bridge was built.

Above: Cadman's Cottage, the oldest dwelling in the City of Sydney. Right: The 'Bounty' at its mooring on Campbell's Cove.

SYDNEY

Previous pages: *The massive arch of Sydney Harbour Bridge spans the channel between Milsons Point and Dawes Point.*

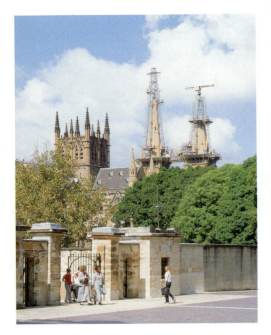

Above: *Government House is the official residence of the Governor of New South Wales.*

Above: *The spires of St Mary's Cathedral were completed in the year 2000, over 130 years after the start of construction.*

Right: *Hyde Park Convict Barracks is now a museum.*

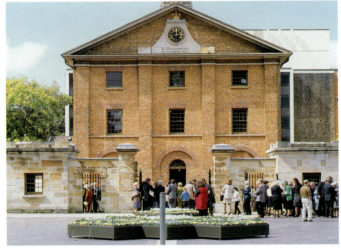

Above left: *The Shrine of Remembrance in Hyde Park. Sculptures by Raynor Hoff evoke the tragedy and toil of the First World War.*
Right: *Terraces in Paddington were built before the age of the automobile.*

THE CITY

Following pages: *City skyscrapers make a towering backdrop to the wharves at Circular Quay.*

Above: *Motorists enjoy a view of the tower of Sydney Town Hall as they drive south on York Street.*

Left: *The cavernous interior of the Queen Victoria Building, a nineteenth century shopping arcade.*

Above: *Historic buildings still line George Street in The Rocks.*
Right: *The Queen Victoria Building, originally a market, then converted to offices, is now shops once more.*

The Beaches

Above: *A brilliant red sky heralds the dawn at Long Reef on Sydney's Northern Beaches.*

Right Page: *Sydney's Northern Beaches stretch into the distance from Manly.*

Below: *A beautiful summer morning at Bronte on Sydney's Southern Beaches.*

If you enjoy a day at the beach, Sydney is the place for you. When I looked at the map to check how many beaches there were, I found that including those on Broken Bay, Sydney Harbour and Royal National Park the tally came to 132. That means you could go to a different beach every Sunday for two and a half years and still have some left for a rainy day.

Sydney beaches range from the world famous such as Bondi and Manly, to those no one has heard of like Werrong Beach and Little Wobby Beach, to those that fill one with a sense of eager anticipation on the way because they may not be there at all, like Washaway Beach and Mackenzie's Bay where the sand may have been scoured away by the last storm. It comes back though.

As you lie prone on the sand lulled into a comatose state by the rush of the waves in your ears and the warm sun on your face, you may care to reflect on how some of the beaches received their names. Palm Beach and Avalon by developers anxious to sell real-estate, Malabar and Collaroy after steamers that came to grief, Rose Bay and Nelson Bay after English lords, and Dee Why where nobody can quite remember why.

For safety don't forget to swim between the flags, have plenty to drink on a hot day so you don't become dehydrated, and remember the sunscreen.

SYDNEY

Previous pages: Manly Beach.

Above: Palm Beach. The ocean is on the left and Pittwater on the right.

Below: From Manly Wharf it's five minute's walk to the ocean.

Above: Freshwater (foreground) and Curl Curl are the next two beaches north of Manly.

Above left: Sunrise at Avalon Beach. The beach was named by a real estate developer in the 1920s.
Above right: A 15 minute walk along a path at the south end of Manly Beach takes you to Shelly Beach.

THE BEACHES

Above: Colourful surf boats during a carnival at North Cronulla.

Below: Early morning surfers at Newport Beach.

Above: A sculpture at Tamarama Beach during the annual 'Sculpture by the Sea' exhibition.

Above right: All eyes are on the surfboats during a carnival at Manly.
Above: Watching the surfers at Queenscliff at the north end of Manly Beach.

Sydney

Left: *A stormy morning at South Cronulla Beach.*

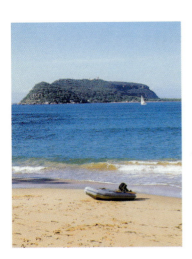

Left: *Quiet Resolute Beach on Pittwater is only accessible by water or on foot.*

Above: *Coogee was the only Sydney beach to ever have a pier. It was demolished in the 1930s.*

Above left: *Sydney's most popular beach, world famous Bondi, attracts daily crowds of 50,000 in summer.*
Above right: *Bronte, Tamarama and Bondi beaches. A track leads from Bondi, round the headlands, to the park at Bronte.*

THE BEACHES

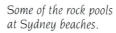
Some of the rock pools at Sydney beaches.

Above: Excitement during rough seas at North Curl Curl.

Above: A colourful dawn sky at Coogee Rock Pool.

Centre: The pool at Bondi Icebergs Club. Above left: The children's pool at Dee Why.
Above right: The pools are rinsed with fresh seawater at high tide. This is Mahon Pool at Maroubra.

The Bush

Just about anywhere in Australia more than 50 kilometers from the nearest town is vaguely referred to as 'the bush'. There may not be any bushes there, it's just called 'the bush'. Though having made that qualification, it is in fact true to say that the countryside around Sydney has bushes, millions and millions of them.

Partly through luck and partly through the energetic campaigning of some dedicated conservationists, unspoilt bush can be found close to the heart of Sydney and in several national parks around the city. Areas around Sydney Harbour reserved for defence, explosives magazines and a quarantine station were released by the Commonwealth Government for public parks when the facilities were no longer required. There's something marvelous about being able to catch a ferry from Circular Quay to Taronga Zoo Wharf and to walk through the bush at Bradleys Head with a view through the trees of the city skyscrapers and harbour.

Further afield Royal National Park on Sydney's southern boundary was set aside in 1879 'for the use of the public forever as a national park' by the Premier Sir John Robertson. It is the oldest national park in the world but at the time of its creation its intended use was 'for military manoeuvres, recreation and camping grounds, or for plantations of ornamental trees and shrubs'.

To explore Ku-ring-gai Chase National Park directly north of the city, maps are available at the park entry and at the Visitors' Centre on Bobbin Head Road. But to really get away from it all, head for the Blue Mountains two hours drive west of Sydney, which has some of the most dramatic scenery and some of the best walks anywhere in Australia. The Blue Mountains have recently received a World Heritage listing as a wilderness area.

Above: Waratahs in bloom. These scarlet flowers are the symbol of New South Wales. Their fiery blooms can be found in the bush around Sydney in September, particularly in Brisbane Waters National Park.

Left: In Sydney virgin bush can still be found close to the city centre. This rainforest gully is at Mosman on the north shore of the harbour, on the walk from Mosman Wharf to Cremorne Point.

THE BUSH

Right and following pages: *The Three Sisters at Katoomba in the Blue Mountains.*

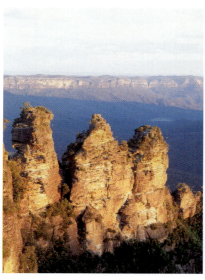

Left: *Early morning mist photographed from Govetts Leap.*

Above: *A low morning sun casts shadows into the Grose Valley. On the walk from Govetts Leap to Pulpit Rock.*
Right: *Mist in the Jamieson Valley. A view from the Valley of the Waters walk at Wentworth Falls.*

SYDNEY

Right: *Rainforest at the start of the Grand Canyon walk.*

Below: *Federal Pass on the track from Katoomba to the Ruined Castle.*

Above left: *Ferns line much of the Grand Canyon walk at Blackheath.*
Right: *Lady Carrington Walk in Royal National Park.* Centre: *Palms on the Forest Path in Royal National Park.*

THE BUSH

Right: Sulphur-crested Cockatoos are often found in flocks of 12 to 20 birds.

Below: The tiny Blue Wren is surprisingly tame and unafraid.

Right: The laughing Kookaburra is a member of the kingfisher family.

Above: A Grey Kangaroo and joey. Common in the bush outside Sydney, this one is at Koala Park sanctuary.
Above right: The female koala is identified by the white fur on its chest. Also photographed at Koala Park.

SYDNEY

Right: *National Falls in Royal National Park.*

Below: *Somersby Falls near Brisbane Waters National Park.*

Above left: *Access to Lower Somersby Falls is by a set of stone steps and a boardwalk.*
Above right: *The twin drop of Katoomba Falls in full flood. Photographed from Furber Steps.*

THE BUSH

Right: Kangaroo Paw, a native wildflower of Western Australia, also grows well in the Sydney region.

Below: Waratahs in bloom. This spectacular flowering shrub seems to thrive on the poor soils of the NSW tablelands and coast.

Below: One of the numerous varieties of banksia shrubs.

Above: Flannel flowers are the symbol of the Warringah district of Sydney. Above right: Orange kangaroo paw.
Following page: Looking down the Bradfield Highway to Sydney Harbour Bridge and the City.